Fern's Story

From Flat Irons to Perma Press, She's Come a Long Way

*...choose for yourselves this day whom you will serve,...
but as for me and my house, we will serve the Lord.*

Joshua 24:15

LISA DONELSON

Copyright © 2020 by Lisa Donelson

ISBN: 978-1-7352570-2-0
Fern's Story
Published by Speak Life

Donelson, Lisa, 1962-
Fern's Story: From Flat Irons to Perma Press, She's Come a Long Way/ Lisa Donelson.
ISBN: 978-1-7352570-2-0
1.Biography.   2. United States - History I. Title
920

All Scripture quotations taken from the New King James Version®. Copyright © 1982 by Thomas Nelson. Used by permission. All rights reserved.

All rights reserved. No part of this book may be reproduced or transmitted in any form or by any means, electronic or mechanical, including photocopying and recording, or by any information storage and retrieval system, without permission in writing from the publisher.

Cover Photos:
Top Center: Fern age 85
Bottom Left: Fern's first Sunday School Class;
Bottom Right: Fern and her dog Sport beside a hay pile

Contents

Growing Up	6
School Days	17
The War Years	23
Married Life	31
The Later Years	53
The Rest of the Story	63

The story of

Fern Hartfiel Sweeter

As told to her daughter
Lisa Donelson
March 2007

Growing Up

Fern was born on March 19, 1922, to George and Ester Hartfiel. She was born at home on the farm the second of three children. Ester was her dad's second wife. His first wife had died, leaving him with a daughter Ellen from his first marriage. When George and Ester married, Ester became Ellen's mama. George and Ester had a son Willard, then a daughter Fern, and finally, another daughter Inez, who died when she was two years old of whooping cough, and pneumonia.

Mom tells stories about her amazing little sister Inez. She could speak both English and German by the time she was two years old. She knew she was supposed to speak German at home, and English at church and in town. She talked about how Inez would help Ellen with the dishes. Ellen would be singing a hymn and forget the words, then Inez would tell her what came next. One time, when Inez was singing the hymn *My Father is rich*, her mama told Inez her father wasn't rich, to which Inez replied, "My Papa isn't rich, but my Father is." At two years old she knew she was a child of the King and belonged to Jesus. The rest of us will look forward to meeting Inez in heaven one day.

Mom was a farm girl through and through. Her parents made their living by farming. She has a lot of stories to tell about how it was to farm in the 1930s with horses and the work of their hands. She tells about getting up about 5:00 am to milk the cows by hand and gather the eggs. Mom and Ellen did some of the milking. The cows always had to be milked twice a day. She told me a funny story about a cow that was a kicker. This cow would always kick over the milk bucket. Ellen had heard if you played a radio in the barn it would calm the cows and they wouldn't kick. Well, they didn't have a radio for the barn, but they could sing. Ellen thought she and Mom should sing so the cow wouldn't kick. Mom held the bucket while Ellen milked the cow and they both sang. The old cow kicked anyway and kicked over the bucket. It was the first and last time they tried that!

She tells about shocking oats and rye by hand and stacking hay on the hay wagon with a pitchfork. They didn't have many machines to do the harvesting. On one of the farms they lived on, the owner told them they had to hoe the weeds out of the corn by hand, even though they had horses and a cultivator to do it. They had to shock the corn at harvest time, too. (This meant they had to cut the corn stalks and tie them in a bundle, then stand them up.) Mom remembers having to get the rye shocked on the 4th of July before they could go to the parade in St. Joseph. She also remembers getting an ice cream cone as a treat after the parade.

She tells about one year when her brother Willard was being a little mischievous on the 4th of July. He had some cherry bombs. They lived next to a dirt road. Willard would go and put a cherry bomb in the driving track so when a car came along and rolled over it, the cherry bomb would explode. The driver would think he had a flat tire. He would get out and look, no flat, scratch his head and go on his way. Willard and Fern got a big kick out of it. After the car was gone, Willard would go put out another cherry bomb. Uncle Willard always seemed to be a rather somber farmer, but he did have a sense of humor!

Life was very different then from what it is today. They didn't have a TV, no cell phone, no computer, no internet, no credit cards, and cars and airplanes were not very common. Mom's parents had a Ford Model A but not a TV. They did have a radio they would gather around to listen to as a family. Mom dreamed of having her very own radio program one day. She wanted to sing hymns and give a little story. She had dreams of telling the gospel message over the radio!

She told me, from the time she was little they had family devotions in their home. Her mom would read the Bible in the morning after breakfast. Her dad never learned to read. Then they would kneel by their chairs to have prayer time. After that, they would get up, sing a hymn and go about their work for the day. Mom was blessed to be raised in a Christian home. They attended church every Sunday. All her life she went to Grace Church in St. Cloud. It started out being First Evangelical Church, then it changed to the Evangelical United Brethren Church, and finally to Grace United Methodist Church. Her family was always active in the church. Fern accepted Jesus as her Savior when she was nine years old and was involved in the church all of her life, singing in the choir, and teaching Sunday school. Fern taught the nursery class from the time she was about 18 until she was in her 50's. The nursery class was for babies to children age five.

When she was young, in the summertime, she had to herd the cows. This involved going outside and watching to make sure the cows did not stray too far from the pasture. They did not have a fenced-in area for the cows. If one went too far away, she would have to go chase it back to the herd. She said she would often take her crocheting or her sewing out with her and sit on the ground doing her handwork while watching the cows. You can tell she never had idle hands.

The home was a place with few modern conveniences. No electricity, just oil lamps, no fancy mattresses, just cotton fabric stuffed with straw, no electric or gas cook stove, just wood. No electric irons, just flat irons at first, and then an iron with a gas burner on it. No electric washing machine or clothes dryer, just hand washing, and hanging the clothes on the line to dry. Mom tells about ironing with flat irons. She said you would use two. One to get hot while you ironed with the first. She said at first the iron would be too hot, so you would have to be careful not to scorch the clothes. Then it would cool off and it wouldn't iron. You would have to take the second one, it would be too hot again. From flat irons they went to a gas burner on the iron, it held a more constant temperature, but it was really heavy she said.

Of course in those days there were no perma press (wrinkle-resistant) fabrics, only cotton, and it was all ironed! But it would not be like ironing your wardrobe today. We are not talking about a closet full of clothes for every member of the family. When Mom was growing up, she had one good dress that she wore to church every Sunday, and two or three everyday dresses. She had one pair of shoes while she was growing up. They had to be polished every Saturday night so they would look good for church on Sunday.

She also tells about their gas engine powered ringer washing machine. It was usually located out on the porch where the fumes from the gas engine could get away from the house. But in the winter it was too cold out on the porch. Then the machine was brought into the house and a window was opened to try to get some of the exhaust out. She said it was "kind of smelly though!"

Fern wore bib overalls when she worked out in the fields. She even wore long stockings underneath to protect her legs. It must have been really hot in the summertime. She remembers one time when she stuck her leg with the pitchfork while pitching hay off the wagon. The pitchfork went through her overalls, into her stocking, and then into her leg. She said her mom used Sayman's Salve on the wound to heal it. The salve even drew out a piece of stocking that was in her leg.

In the early years, she remembers they used feed sacks to sew their clothes. When the men went to town to buy feed, they had to be careful to choose matching sacks to get enough of the same kind of fabric. The feed sacks in those days had printed designs on them and were in color so their clothes were not just solid colors. They would purchase large sacks of feed. It took several sacks to make a dress. They were made from rough cotton.

Mom started sewing when she was very young. I have a baby crib spread and a pillow cover she embroidered when she was just six years old. Because she had to go to the dentist, her mama promised her she would buy the set for her to embroider if she was a good girl. It made her really happy to get that crib set to embroider. I'm thinking it would not be the kind of thing today's six-year-old would choose as a treat for being good at the dentist!

She told me when she was little they did not have many toys. She remembers getting one toy at Christmas from her parents, and one from her Grandma and Grandpa Herzberg. One year, she got two dolls, one from her parents and one from her grandparents, she said she pretended she had twins. She also does not remember many books in the house when she was growing up, just one Bible story book. She says maybe that's why she likes books so much now.

Their meals were different from what we eat today too. When Fern was young, there were no prepared foods like Pop-Tarts or flavored oatmeal in a single serving package. For breakfast, they often had fried potatoes and sausage, or plain oatmeal, or bread with cream and brown sugar. She said sometimes they had corn flakes from a box. They had their big meal at noon. They would often have home canned meat, like beef or pork. She said they would put the jar of meat in the hot water reservoir at the back of the wood cook stove and put some potatoes in the oven. When they came in from outside they would have dinner ready. They would use the juice from the meat as their gravy. The meat was cooked when it was canned, it only needed to be warmed up. They would also butcher roosters for chicken meat. For supper, they would have scrambled eggs or egg pancakes. Sometimes they would have creamed cold potatoes or German potato salad.

Clothes were not always in the budget when Mom was growing up. She tells of several times when her brother Willard bought her something she needed. One time there was going to be a sleigh ride at their Uncle Robert's. She couldn't go because all she had to wear were her work overalls, no nice pants or a snowsuit. In those days, if you were going somewhere, overalls were not acceptable. Willard went to town to buy her a nice pair of red pants to wear to the sleigh ride. One year when she was about 19, she needed a new coat, Willard used his money from selling a calf to buy her a new coat. As a graduation gift, Willard bought her a new dress, it was flowered with a white collar on it. Mom remembers Willard as a good brother who always took care of her, even after they were married, and had their own families.

Most of the family had a birthday in March, Fern's was the 19th, Willard's was the 14th, Ellen's was the 26th, and Grandpas was on the 12th. I think the weather was a little different when Mom was growing up. She tells about how they would make sure there was a pile of straw covering a patch of snow. They wanted to have ice to make homemade ice cream for the March birthdays. They always celebrated each person's birthday on the day. When

Mom and Dad got married, Dad was added to the March birthdays, his being on March 22nd. And when Willard got married, they added his wife Eunice, whose birthday was the 3rd of March. When I was growing up, our family always chose a Sunday in March to get together. We would have a meal with cake and ice cream for all the March birthdays.

Mom's family usually had a garden, but Mom commented the fieldwork came before the garden work. The whole family helped in the fields. She said there was no such thing as a sick day on the farm. If you didn't feel good you took an aspirin and went back to work. She says that's how she learned to be tough! When she was little, she had whooping cough and scarlet fever. Ellen had it first, and then Mom got it. Willard didn't get either one. She also remembers one other time when she got sick, she had to clean out a root cellar with rotten potatoes in it. The smell of those potatoes made her really sick.

I asked about their summer vacation. She told me they never had much summer vacation because of the farm work. Their vacation was to go to visit her dad's, Uncle Henry and Aunt Mary. They didn't have any children. Uncle Henry lived in Maple Grove, MN. Grandpa would take the family one Sunday each summer to visit Uncle Henry and Aunt Mary. They would go early enough so they could go to church together, and then go to Uncle

Henry's for lunch. Mom tells a funny story about one particular year. The pew they sat in had a crack in the seat. When they all sat down, the crack opened up, when they stood up, the crack closed. Fern's mother was the last one to get up, her dress got stuck in the crack. She couldn't stand up for the hymn. They all had a chuckle over that.

Visiting Uncle Henry was fun! He would copy what the kids were doing. If they scratched their nose, he would scratch his nose, all while carrying on a conversation with Grandpa. If they crossed their legs, he would cross his legs. Simple fun, but they had a good time! She said in the summer, one Sunday, they would go to Lake Koronis near Paynesville, MN to the church camp for Assembly Sunday. Many of their relatives would also come. They would attend the morning church service, have a big picnic lunch with the family, and then attend the afternoon church service. It was like a family reunion for them. Those few Sundays out visiting their family were all the summer vacation they had, but she said they never thought anything of it. It was just the way it was.

Willard, Ellen, and Fern, taken about 1924. Fern would be about 2 in this photo.

School Days

Mom went to the country school through grade five. She remembers living on five different farms while growing up. In 1929, right before the stock market crash, her dad sold the farm they were living on. He put his money in the bank. His sister worked at the bank, and he thought it was safe there. The bank closed with the stock market crash and he lost all of his money. From that time on, he only rented farms; he never owned land again. His sister felt really bad. She said if she had any idea the bank was going to close, she would have told him, but there was no warning.

The summer before Mom was to start 6th grade, they moved to a farm near St. Joseph. It was five miles to the country school from the new place, too far to walk, and the only other school was the Catholic school in St. Joe. But her family wasn't Catholic, so that wasn't an option. This meant she had to go to St. Cloud to finish her education. Ellen was ten years older than Mom and had finished school. Willard had finished 9th grade and was needed on the farm. Mom was the only one who was young enough to go to school. She stayed with her Grandma and Grandpa Herzberg in St. Cloud, during the week while going to school, and came home on the weekends. She did that from 6th grade until she graduated from Tech High School in 1940.

She went to Washington Elementary School on the south side of St. Cloud, then to South Junior High, which is now the St. Cloud City office building on Division Street. Then to Tech High School for grades 10-12. She is the only one in her family to graduate from high school.

They didn't live on the farm near St. Joseph for very long before moving to a different farm. Everyone said the man who owned this new farm was really hard to get along with and that George and Ester wouldn't last. They told Ester she shouldn't unpack when she got there. Mom said her dad was an easy-going kind of guy. When the owner came to complain about anything, her dad would just listen, and then go about his business. They farmed that place on shares. Her dad would pay a percentage of the income from the crop once a year as rent to the owner. This was in payment for living on the farm and taking care of it. The original owner died, then Albert Hengle bought the farm. Mom's family continued to live there for many years. They ended up living on that farm until both her mom and dad died. Willard rented the farm for a few more years. Finally, Willard bought his own farm near Foley. Her Mom never did get all her boxes unpacked. The house had three bedrooms upstairs and a bedroom, kitchen, and living room on the main floor.

When Mom was a little girl, before she started school in St. Cloud, she would spend a week in the summer at her Grandma's in St. Cloud. Her Grandma Herzberg, her Mom's mother, taught her to crochet, and helped her crochet some edgings around washcloths for Christmas gifts. It was her first crochet project. She also tells about what a treat it was to ride the streetcar to downtown St. Cloud and go to Woolworth's for a strawberry pop.

Her mom taught her to sew, first by hand, and then with the treadle sewing machine. All their dresses and shirts were sewn on the machine, most of them from printed feed sacks. Mom remembers her first sewing machine project was to sew bias tape around the edge of an apron when she was about eight or nine years old. Today we don't even wear aprons, and most young people wouldn't know what bias tape is. Bias tape is used instead of a hem to finish edges. She also remembers making a dress pattern for 4-H, and sewing the dress when she was about 12. When she stayed at her grandma's while going to school, she made a double wedding ring quilt top. She hand-stitched the pieces together.

When she lived with Grandma and Grandpa while going to school, she was expected to cook supper, wash the dishes, and help around the house. She says as her grandparents got older, Grandma couldn't see and Grandpa couldn't hear. She would help them out by repeating what Grandma said to Grandpa, or helping Grandma with the housework. She says she remembers Grandma using a magnifier to do her handwork since her eyesight was so bad. While she was living with Grandma and Grandpa, Fern decided she would never have cats in her own house. Aunt Irma was still living at home and she had cats. The cats would hang on the drapes, hide behind the couch, and jump out at Mom and snag her nylon stockings. Stockings were a little hard to come by, so she never appreciated those cats.

When she was in the 6th grade, the class had a unit on the Vikings. They were all asked to make a project showing something about the Vikings. Mom made a ship out of fabric that she appliqued (fancy stitched) pieces onto. She said most of the others drew pictures or painted a picture. The teacher liked hers so well she offered to buy it from her.

All of her life she has done such nice handwork that she has often been able to sell it to others. She has also given away much of what she has made. She said her mama taught her to always do everything to the best of her ability, as if she were doing it for the Lord.

She also tells about a time when she was in 8th grade Home Economics. They were asked to sew something for a younger brother or sister. Mom didn't have a younger brother or sister, but her friend Vivian had a little brother Jimmy who was about three. She said Vivian's mom gave her the pattern and the material for an outfit for Jimmy. It was a white shirt with blue polka dots and short blue pants that buttoned on. There were a lot of buttonholes. She made them all by hand on the shirt and the pants. She got an A+ on the project. The mothers of the students came in to see all the projects the girls had made. They thought Fern's sewing was so nice they asked the teacher if they could hire her to sew for them. The teacher said, "No, Fern had school work to do."

When she was in high school, her classes were: Algebra, Typing, Shorthand, Office Practice, Home Economics, English, Social Studies, and History. She said she didn't like history at all. She took the business classes because she wanted to be a secretary when she graduated. Her favorite class was Algebra, and she was very good at it. Her teacher, Mr. Lunamen, really liked her. On a test day, he would give the keys to the classroom to Fern, and ask her to put the test on the blackboard during lunch, then she didn't have to take the test. She would often help the other students with their assignments too.

When Fern graduated from High School in 1940, she thought maybe she would be able to get a job as a secretary, but her sister Ellen had other ideas. Ellen had been living at home helping out on the farm and around the house. She was 10 years older than Fern. When Fern was done with school and no longer need to live in town during the week, Ellen decided she was going to be the one leaving home, not Fern. One day she just packed Willard's suitcase and got a ride into St. Cloud to work for a family she knew. She didn't even tell her parents about her plans-- she just left. She later told her mother she couldn't stay on the farm because the dust bothered her too much. Grandma Ester got a big kick out of it when Ellen later married a farmer!

Fern on graduation day!

The War Years

Fern lived at home from 1940 to 1946. She loved her family, and even if the work was hard, it was just what had to be done. During those years between high school and marriage, Fern did a lot of handwork. She helped out on the farm, in the house, in the garden, and in the field. In the evenings she crocheted a large table cloth out of crochet cotton by lamplight. If you have ever seen the difference between a kerosene lamp, and an electric light, you would know she had good eyesight in those days. She got her first permanent wave during those years. Ellen gave her money for her birthday so she could go to the beauty shop to get a permanent wave. It wasn't done with rollers and solution; it was done with rollers connected to wires. The rollers were clamped on your hair. An electrical charge was used to 'wave' the hair. She said one time her head got burned!

Fern's whole family enjoyed music. She tells a story about gas rationing during the war. Their family had enough gas to go to church on Sunday, and for the tractor, but not enough to go to choir practice at church in St. Cloud during the week. The pastor, or one of the ladies in the choir with a car, would load up the rest of the choir members and drive out to their house for choir practice.

Since Mom's family all sang in the choir it worked out really well.

She tells a story about one time when her mother was sick and had to go to the hospital in Rochester. She wanted to do a really good job of taking care of the house while her mother was gone. So she got busy one morning and mixed up a batch of bread, she got it ready for the oven, then started doing some housework. She wanted to take down the curtains to wash and iron them. She put her bread in the oven after it had risen, then went about washing and ironing curtains. When it was time for supper, she went to put the bread on the table, but it was still in the oven - burned black. She felt really bad, but we all know, sometimes we forget things!

Not long after she graduated from high school, the United States entered World War II. Fern remembers writing letters to a lot of the boys in the service. She remembers Irvin Scheel thought she was pretty special. But once she met Walter, she knew there was something special about him. She didn't meet him until after he got home from the war in 1945. Walter attended Graham Church in Rice, a sister church to Grace Church in St. Cloud, where Mom went to church. He had a picture of the church youth group someone had sent him when he was overseas. He particularly liked the looks of one young lady and hoped she was not taken when he got back. That young lady was Fern. Walter asked if he could take her home from the young peoples' New Year's Eve party on New Year's Eve of 1945. Fern had come to the party with her brother Willard, so she asked him if it was okay if Walter took her home, Willard said sure. That was the beginning of a whirlwind courtship.

Walter wasted no time in finding out if Fern was the girl for him. After only a few dates he asked her if she intended to get married or if she was going to be an old maid. She said she would like to get married someday. By March of 1946, they were engaged. On the night Dad asked Mom to marry him, he fell asleep behind the wheel of his Hudson and rolled the car, making it impossible to drive. So, from then on, he was on foot or riding the bus to go and visit Fern on the farm.

They couldn't get married until fall, because she had promised her brother Willard she would help him with the harvest. They set the wedding date for November 16, 1946. It ended up being her Grandma and Grandpa Herzberg's wedding anniversary.

Although they didn't date very long, Walter was a faithful suitor, even without a car. He was working for the railroad out of St. Cloud and living in Sauk Rapids with his Aunt Martha. After work, he would ride the streetcar from Sauk Rapids to St. Cloud and then out to Waite Park.

When he got to the end of the streetcar line, he would walk out to Fern's to visit her for the evening, at least once a week. He also joined the church choir, just so he could see her in the middle of the week. Anyone who ever heard Dad sing could only call it a joyful 'noise'. He always loved to sing, but because of his hearing trouble, he really couldn't carry a tune. Even Fern's brother Willard, who stood next to him at choir practice told her once, "Boy, that Walter really can't sing!" As soon as they were married, Dad stopped singing in the choir!

Even before they were married, Fern and Walter read the Bible together. She told me one of the verses they liked was Romans 8:31. *What then shall we say to these things? If God is for us, who can be against us?* They knew God was with them, and would always help them, no matter what challenges they faced.

Fern's sister Ellen did not want to be an old maid. She wasted no time finding a husband herself. She met Henry and they decided to marry. Mom suggested they have a double wedding. Ellen didn't like the idea. She set her wedding date for January 1, 1947. Just a few weeks after Fern and Walter's. Fern, of course, needed a wedding dress for her wedding. Since it was just after the war was over, there was not a wedding dress in her size to be found in St. Cloud. One day, she and Ellen took the bus to Minneapolis to shop for a wedding dress. After going to several stores. She found a very nice white taffeta dress with a train and a crinoline underskirt for $25. She kept that dress. I wore it for my wedding 39 years later.

Fern and Walter on their wedding day.

Mom and Dad's wedding day dawned cold and clear, but they had some snow showers before the day was over. They were married in the Evangelical United Brethren Church in St. Cloud, the same church that would later be Grace United Methodist. This was the same church Mom had been raised in, and her parents had attended all the years she was growing up. It was also the same church where she sang in the choir and taught Sunday school. As she walked down the aisle, one of her little Sunday school children whispered "That's my teacher!" Mom's sister Ellen and Dad's sister Jessie were Mom's attendants. Mom's brother Willard and Dad's cousin Sam, stood up with him. After the wedding, they had the reception in the basement of the church. Walter had planned for them to take a wedding trip on the train, out west to visit his family. They had to hurry after the wedding to catch the train, and they forgot to cut the wedding cake! No one had any wedding cake that day. They didn't want to cut it since the bride and groom hadn't done it. When they got back from their wedding trip two weeks later, there was the whole cake at Mom's parent's house.

While growing up, we often heard the 'mouse' story from the train ride out west. Walter got free tickets since he worked for the railroad. They stayed with Walter's family at every stop. On the first night as they were riding along after dark, Fern was sitting in her seat, a new bride, suddenly a mouse ran up her arm. She just sort of squeaked, "Walter, a mouse ran up my arm!" Walter was impressed with his new bride, he thought any other woman would have screamed so loud, everyone on the train would have panicked. It wasn't that Fern wasn't scared, she just didn't yell.

Their first stop was Salt Lake City, Utah, to visit Walter's brother, Sandy, and his wife Shirley. Then Sandy and Shirley drove them to California to visit his dad and his stepmother, and his younger sisters, Esther, Delores, Anna, and Martha. Fern said it was quite a ride. While Sandy was driving on the mountain roads at night, his headlights went out on his car. Thankfully, he decided to stop for the night and try to find a garage that could fix the car in the morning. The next day was Sunday, so they had to wait until noon for the gas station to open to get the lights fixed.

Dad's little sister Martha was quite young. She didn't know if she liked Mom being married to her older brother. Fern would put her hair up every night. Martha saw her with her hair in curlers, she asked if she let Walter see her like that. Fern thought it was kind of cute. They got back on the train in California. They traveled up the coast to Oregon to visit more family. Walter's sister Minnie and her husband Wesley Bloom, and his brother

Clarence and his wife Daisy. From there they came home on the train. Their trip lasted about two weeks.

Fern and Walter in front of their second house in town.

Married Life

When they came home, their first house was a single car garage. Housing was hard to find in St. Cloud after the war. Mom remembers it was about a 12 x 18 garage. It was one room. They had a table and chairs for the kitchen, with a three burner kerosene cook stove, a sink, and a kitchen cupboard. The kitchen cupboard separated the kitchen from the bed in the 'bedroom', where they had a small dresser in the corner. They had a sewing machine her Uncle Robert had given her and a little wood stove for heat. They didn't have much money. She said they ate a lot of tomato soup.

Mom told me a story about one of the first years they were married. She wanted a new dress for Easter Sunday, but they didn't have money to buy one, or even to buy fabric. Instead, she remodeled one of her old dresses. She got out her spring coat and was all ready for Easter Sunday. Then it snowed and she had to put her spring coat away and wear her winter coat instead. She was kind of disappointed.

At first, they didn't have a refrigerator. They put the food that needed to be chilled outside in the well. One day Fern took the bus to downtown St. Cloud to go shopping. At Herberger's, a local department store, they were having a flash sale on refrigerators. You had to buy it now, or not get the sale price of $10. She bought it without asking Walter. She was a little nervous at first, not knowing if he would approve or not. She says she can't quite remember how she got the refrigerator home, but it was good to have a refrigerator.

They were happy in their little garage. Dad would walk to work because they didn't have a car yet. They did have a telephone. Mom remembers when Dad's Grandma Sweeter called her one day soon after they were married. Mom answered the phone, and Grandma said, "Hello Mrs. Sweeter? This is Mrs. Sweeter." It made Mom chuckle. On Sundays, Uncle Robert would take them to church and then they would go home with Mom's parents for lunch. Willard would bring them back into town at the end of the day.

Walter had ordered a new car after he rolled his Hudson the night they were engaged. Cars were hard to get after the war. It took a long time to get one. While they were waiting for the new car to come in, one of the guys who worked with Walter found out he had a new car on order. This guy had a Ford Model A car, he asked Walter if he would like to buy his Model A. This guy would then buy Walter's new car when it came in. Mom and Dad thought it sounded like a good idea since the Model A would not be as expensive as a new car. When the new car was ready, they bought the Model A and the other guy bought their new car.

Mom had never learned to drive, so Dad set out to teach her to drive the Model A. She was driving one day and went in the ditch. She almost hit a mailbox. That scared her, so she didn't try driving again for many years. After they moved to the farm, they had a little Rambler station wagon with a push-button shift. Mom was learning to drive it. Then one foggy night Dad was coming home from Uncle Willard's on the country roads. He was following the electric highline poles because he couldn't see the road. The only problem was, the electric highline poles went straight, but the road turned. Once again Mom didn't have a car to drive. She gave up learning to drive after that.

Since housing was hard to find after the war, Walter bought another small garage across the alley from them in town. They rented it out for a while. After a year or so, they were able to buy a partially completed house not far from where they were living. The house was framed in but not finished inside. They decided to buy the house and rent out both garages. In the evenings, Walter would come home and tack up a few sheets of sheetrock inside the house, then when he was gone to work the next day, Fern would finish nailing them up.

Before long they sold both of the small garage houses and put the money toward the new house. They lived in that house for 16 years, until they bought the farm out in the country. They traded the house in town for part of the payment on the farm and borrowed the rest. They never borrowed money from a bank for any of their houses. The money they needed for their houses was always borrowed from a private party.

When they first got married, they decided they wanted to be tithers, and they would have morning devotions together every day. They faithfully gave ten percent of their income to the church. Mom said there were some weeks when they thought they might need to use the tithe money for bills, but they never did. God always took care of their needs. They were faithful with their morning devotions as well, and as the children came along they added evening Bible stories after supper. Mom and Dad's home was always one where God was honored, the Bible respected, and weekly attendance at church was a part of life.

Not long after Mom and Dad were married, Mom's mother died. She died on April 29, 1948. She had gotten sick, and fluid filled up in her lungs. The doctor was not able to help her. She died at home. Mom and Dad were able to visit her the night before she died. Mom always talked about her mother with so much love. I know she missed having her to talk to about many things in her married life.

In July of 1949, they had their first baby. A boy, Ralph George Sweeter. The middle name, George, was after Fern's dad. Ralph was a joy to their home. He was a smart little boy. There are a lot of Ralph stories when he was growing up. Fern read to him a lot. Since he liked books, she would read Bible stories to him. One of their preachers liked to hear Ralph say Nebuchadnezzar when he was just beginning to talk. He could say it real clear too.

There are several fishing stories with Ralph. In those early days, Dad liked to fish and Mom would sometimes go along. Ralph would go too when he was a toddler. One summer they were out in the boat fishing and Ralph was taking a nap. When he woke up from his nap, Mom gave him a Tootsie Roll. She had a few in her pocket for him as treats. He slowly unwrapped the Tootsie Roll, and in his half-asleep state, tossed the Tootsie Roll into the lake. It didn't take long for him to realize he threw away the wrong thing, "My Tootsie Roll!" he cried! Mom, of course, had another. Then there is the time they went ice fishing in the winter. Ralph was along, he was getting tired and wanted to go home. He had heard about another little boy who had accidentally stuck his foot in the fishing hole, and got all wet. The parents took him home. Ralph thought it might just work for him, so he stuck his foot in the hole on purpose. Of course, Mom and Dad knew what he was up to. Ralph only got as far as the car, not all the way home. He had to sit in the car and wait for them to be ready to go home.

In October of 1951, their second child came to join the family. A baby boy, James Walter Sweeter. He was not to be with them for long though. He was a fussy baby. Mom took him to the doctor and spent many hours with him. The doctors discovered he had leukemia. They had never seen it in such a small baby. They said he got it after he was born, but he only lived a little over a month. He died November 26, 1951. That year was especially hard for Mom. Not only did her baby die, but also her favorite uncle, Robert, and Walter's Grandpa and Grandma Sweeter. Grandma Sweeter died in October, the same month James was born, then, baby James died. Uncle Robert died in January, her Dad died in March, and Grandpa Sweeter died in April. Through it all, God was her refuge and strength. She always told me God knew how much she loved babies, so he is keeping one in heaven for her.

After baby James, there were three miscarriages, and then baby LeRoy. LeRoy John Sweeter was born in August of 1956. They gave him the middle name John because John means "gift from God" and because it was Grandpa Sweeter's name. Mom had spent most of her pregnancy on bed rest since the doctor was concerned she would miscarry again. But God had a plan for LeRoy, and he was born into a loving Christian home.

When LeRoy was about two or three, he had a little red wagon. He decided he wanted a Popsicle. He knew they sold Popsicles at the local store called Winks, about two or three blocks down the street. He set off with his wagon to get a Popsicle. He neglected to tell Mom where he was going or what he was going to do. Mom lost track of him. She went outside to see where he went. She saw him down the block, ready to cross a busy street with his wagon. She ran to the end of the block and caught him before he could cross. She asked him what he was doing, he said he was going to get a Popsicle. He got a spanking for that! I don't know who was more upset, LeRoy, or Mom. She was really scared that such a little boy would set out on his own through town for a Popsicle.

When Fern and Walter lived in town, they had a homemade camper Walter had built. The frame was steel, he built the box for it out of plywood. He was always building something. He really enjoyed creating things. It had bunks inside, a cupboard for food storage, and a hot plate to cook on. One summer they took a trip to Carlton, MN to Jay Cook State Park to go agate hunting. LeRoy and Ralph were young at the time. Fern had sewn black and white checked shirts for the whole family. She made shirts for the boys and Walter, and a blouse for herself. When they went into a restaurant to eat, the waitress commented on how good the family looked all dressed alike. On Sunday they went to church in Carlton. Even on vacation, they did not want to miss out on going to church. They went to Sunday school too. An older couple in the congregation invited them to come home with them for Sunday dinner. Ralph had a Sunday school paper with a story that was continued the following Sunday. The nice lady sent the next week's Sunday school paper to Ralph in the mail so he could finish the story.

Fern had a neighbor in town, Mrs. Ficker. She was a very nice friendly lady who shared a lot of things with Mom. She gave her recipes, and visited with her. She was an older lady. She and Mom got along very well. She would send over fresh hot rolls some mornings just at breakfast time. She is also the one who got Mom started with her violets. Mrs. Ficker would give her a plant, or a leaf that was started. Mom has had violets for many years. Mom remembers Mrs. Ficker putting on her dress and going to church every morning. She was a devout Catholic. I'm sure God sent Mrs. Ficker into Mom's life to help fill the gap of her own mother not being with her any longer.

About a year before they moved to the farm, Fern started selling Avon in her neighborhood in St. Cloud. She was the neighborhood Avon lady. It wasn't the last time she would embark on a career as an Avon lady. She sold Avon again in the '80s in the area around the farm. Her career in St. Cloud was kind of short, when she got pregnant with me (Lisa) she had to quit because the fragrances made her sick. When she sold Avon out in the country, she took over an Avon route I started during one of my summers between college years. I guess you could say I got her out of Avon, and then back in to it again! She made lots of friends in both of those neighborhoods when she sold Avon. When they moved to the farm, the neighborhood ladies in town had a party for her, and gave her lots of nice gifts. When she sold Avon in the country, Dad was retired. He would drive her around on her route. Some of the ladies said she was the best Avon Lady they had ever had.

Just six weeks before Fern and Walter moved to the farm, they had me, baby Lisa. I was born in December of 1962 and they moved in January. I was the girl Mom didn't think she could have. When the nun at the hospital told her she had a girl, she said "It can't be, I only have boys." Of course, she was still a little drugged. When she knew for sure it was a girl, she was glad.

The farmhouse they moved to, thankfully, had an indoor bathroom, not very common for farmhouses in the area at the time. Most of those old houses still had outhouses in the yard. The house was not heated very well. Baby Lisa got whooping cough and was very sick. They had to sit up with me at night in the small bathroom, the only room in the house they could heat sufficiently. Not many weeks after they moved out to the farm, several of the church people pitched in to help them. One was a heating contractor, and another helped with the expense of putting in a hot water boiler and hot water baseboard heaters throughout the house. Mom and Dad were very thankful for the help of their church friends.

When Mom and Dad moved to the farm in 1963, Mom got lonely. She was used to having neighbors close by, and being able to call her friends. Out in the country, St. Cloud was a long-distance phone call, and they had a party line. One ring is for you, two rings are for your neighbor, one long ring is for someone else. The interesting thing about the party line is, if two people were talking on the phone, a third person on the party line could pick up their receiver and hear the conversation. Only one person on the party line could make a call at a time. Fern's brother Willard would call her sometimes and talk German to her, which she could still understand, but she forgot how to speak most of it. She had a hard time putting sentences together to talk back to him! They spoke German so others on the party line wouldn't know what they were talking about. Her only company during the day was baby Lisa. Eventually, the phone became a private party phone, and there was no longer a charge to call long-distance to St.Cloud.

LeRoy had started kindergarten the year before Mom and Dad moved to the farm. On the day they moved, he was told to go to the neighbors after school. He didn't. He went home instead, and sat in the corner of the empty house and cried. He got over it though and enjoyed life on the farm. He had horses, and dogs, and all kinds of things to do outside. He was involved in 4-H. He even started the dog training project with the local 4-H club. Mom remembers one day when LeRoy was riding his horse around the yard. The horse decided it wanted to go in the barn. The barn door was really low, Mom was watching from the kitchen window. She got kind of nervous when she saw that horse headed into the barn with LeRoy on its back, but LeRoy just laid down backward on the horse and rode it in!

Ralph was 13 and LeRoy was 6, when Mom and Dad moved. I guess Dad felt it was time for his boys to have a taste of county life where they could have horses, and animals, and a garden. We had all of that. Always a garden, horses, pigs, a cow for butchering, and for a time, chickens. Always a few cats, and various dogs. One time LeRoy brought a cat home from school on the bus in a paper bag. He got it from the preacher at Religious Release Time. In those days, once a week, students were allowed to leave the public school to attend religious classes at a church for a few hours. That cat was always called 'the preacher's cat'! Another time, we brought two kittens home from Arkansas. They were cute, long-haired cats. Of course, a long-haired cat couldn't be found in Minnesota! But the cats were never welcome inside the house!

Since Dad worked for the railroad, he got paid vacation time every summer. Some summers we would all go to Arkansas in the car to visit Dad's two sisters, Anna and Martha, and Anna's family. The first year Fern and Walter made this trip, Walter didn't think they could drive all the way in one day. So they packed up their '51 Chevy, and the two boys, Ralph and LeRoy, and tied a sheet of plywood on top of the car. The plan was, they would drive most of the day and then stop along the road for the night. The boys would sleep on the seats, bench seats of course. Dad would put the plywood inside the car across the top of the seat, and he and Mom would sleep on it. Walter was always frugal, no hotel for him! It was summertime, and really hot. There wasn't much room between the seats and the roof of the car. They couldn't leave the windows open for air, because the mosquitos would get in, and Ralph was allergic to mosquito bites. They did not get much sleep that night! By the next night, they had arrived in Arkansas.

On the way home, the plywood blew off of the car on the first day. Walter said, "Let it go!" He never did turn around to pick it up. I guess it was one of his plans that didn't work out as well as he had hoped! On later trips, they would start early enough in the morning, usually, about 3:00 AM to make it to Arkansas before the end of the day. It was usually about a 13-14 hour trip in those days before freeways, with the only stops being for gas and food at the same time. We didn't go every summer, but there were several trips to Arkansas over the years. One year Mom even packed an anniversary cake in the trunk. Anna and Arnold were celebrating their 25th wedding anniversary. Mom had been baking and decorating cakes for a while. She thought she would like to bake their cake and decorate it. She baked the three-tiered cake and packed it in separate layers in the trunk, along with our luggage. Mom's sister Ellen and her husband Henry also went with us on this trip. When we got to Arkansas, Mom assembled the cake and put the finishing touches on the decorating.

Several times a year the "Missy Man" would come calling when they lived in the country. This was a traveling salesman. Everyone in the neighborhood called him the "Missy Man" because he called every lady "Missy". He would drive around the neighborhood with a suitcase full of items. He would knock on doors and ask if he could show his goods. In his suitcase would be things like aspirin, or hairpins, or some small toys for children, things people might be out of and need. His prices were reasonable. Sometimes Mom would buy something, but generally, she got all her shopping done on Friday night in St. Cloud.

For as long as I can remember Friday night was shopping night. Every Friday night after Dad came home from work, we would have supper and then go shopping in St. Cloud. At the time it was the only night of the week the stores were open late, and then only until 9:00 PM. The other nights they were only open until 5:00. No 24-hour Walmart back then!

One summer there was a particularly bad summer thunderstorm. Fern was in the kitchen, Ralph and LeRoy were upstairs, and Lisa was playing by Fern. She saw the sky turn very dark and greenish, and heard a loud noise.

She picked Lisa up, called for the boys to come downstairs, and everyone went down in the basement. She heard what sounded like large hail and very strong wind. When they came upstairs later, the corn crib was blown over, and the crops in the garden and the field were all flattened. Mom was sure it was a tornado. She was thankful there was no damage to the house. The sheltering hill the house was built next to protected it from many storms, and of course, God was always watching over them. The storm did not get to St. Cloud. When Walter got home he was really surprised to see all the damage.

Fern always kept busy with her handwork. She was always crocheting, or knitting, or sewing. She sewed a lot of her clothes, and clothes for her children too. She even sewed several men's suits. For a long time, she would knit and sew Barbie doll clothes, for Lisa when she was little and for others. Walter's sister Jessie worked as a telephone operator in St. Cloud. Fern would knit little sweaters, and skating outfits, and sew Barbie dresses and Ken clothes. Jessie would take them to work and sell them for her. Then she started crocheting outfits for plastic baby dolls. They were so popular she had to buy the dolls by the box full. She crocheted boy and girl outfits in all the colors of the rainbow, and then, in her ever-creative way, branched off into other patterns which she designed. A football player, a clown, Santa and Mrs. Claus, the Pilgrims, Indians, a bunny outfit for Easter, a baseball player. She made a whole bunch of Arkansas Razor Back football players for Aunt Anna to sell in her beauty shop in Gravett, Arkansas.

After Dad retired, she started crocheting her famous Christmas angels. The family would often tease her about having a new model each year! One Christmas she crocheted 300 angels. That was the year Fern and Walter were helping their church raise money for their new building. She was crocheting angels for Jesus! She also crocheted all kinds of little things for every holiday. They would make their regular rounds to many places of busi-

Some of Fern's wall hangings. These are done in Filet Crochet,
a series of open and closed squares.
She designed the one with the cross and the lamb.

ness where the employees would buy Mom's work. Then she would take orders from people. They would call her and order whatever they wanted. She also finished several large projects for people. One was a bedspread for one of the cousins in Texas.

Walter had a cousin, Lester. His mother had started a crocheted bedspread before she died but she never finished it. Lester and Eileen wanted to use it, so they asked Fern to finish it. She did, and it turned out beautifully. I truly believe Mom's talent with her handwork is a gift from God. She has used it since she was a little girl, and God has blessed it. She started crocheting banners for the church in the late 1980s. She finished her most recent one the year before she died. She has designed her own patterns and used patterns from books. She has always been very creative.

In the summer of 1965, Fern told Walter she thought they ought to have a family reunion for his brothers and sisters and their families. There were nine children in Dad's family. His sister Minnie died young. His sisters Jessie and Martha never married. Jessie was the only one who lived close to them in Sauk Rapids. Clarence and Daisy with their three children lived in Oregon. Sandy and Shirley and their five children lived in Arizona. Anna and Arnold with their two boys, along with Dad's sister Martha, lived in Arkansas. Delores and her son Kit lived in Arkansas at the time, and Dad's sister Esther lived in California with her four children. Many aunts and uncles lived in the St. Cloud area. None of Dad's brothers and sisters had ever been to visit Fern and Walter in a long time. They were on the farm now and had lots of room for the family to come for a visit. The last time Walter saw some of his family was on their wedding trip 20 years ago. Travel was not as easy in those days. Airline tickets were expensive, and people did not travel as much as they do today. The dates were set and the plans were made.

They all managed to get to Minnesota with their families that summer in July. Most of them drove. Walter had just built a new shop with a cement floor. They set up cots in the shop for the boys, and cots in the garage for the girls. They used every room in the house and then some to accommodate all of the family. Fern planned her menus ahead of time, and she was really glad she did. She baked pies ahead and made as much food as possible ahead of time. For three weeks or more, she spent most of her day in the kitchen, cooking breakfast, cleaning up, getting ready for lunch, fixing lunch, cleaning up, fixing supper, and cleaning up. Then the brothers and sisters would stay up until midnight telling stories. Fern didn't want to miss out on visiting with the family. She stayed up late, only to get up again the next morning at about 6:00 AM to start breakfast for the boys. All of the cousins remember that time in Minnesota. It was one of the few times they were all together. Dad's family had another family reunion five years later in Arkansas, but by then, some of the older children were already working or gone from home. They moved the family reunions up to every three years and had them for many years.

Ralph was 17 the year they had the first family reunion. He was already working for the Northern Pacific railroad at the time. Ralph married Cathy in December of that year and they had baby Jimmy, in April, Mom's first grandson. Some might say Ralph and Cathy got married too young. I don't know what happened, but their marriage didn't last. By the time Jimmy was four, Ralph and Cathy were divorced, Jimmy, lived with Mom and Dad for a time. Ralph met Sue, and they lived at Mom and Dad's for a while before they got married. It was a difficult time for Mom and Dad. In the late 1960's, getting divorced was not as acceptable as it is today. The moral values of that time were different. Fern and Walter were dedicated Christians, and Ralph was not choosing to walk with God and live according to God's Word. But they loved their son, and wanted to help him any way they could. By the time Jimmy was five, Cathy had gotten custody of Jimmy. Ralph chose to let her raise him. He thought it was best for Jimmy not to be bounced back and forth between two families. Mom did not give up though, she always sent Jimmy cards for his birthday and special days. Jimmy told her one time he always knew which Halloween card was from his Grandma Sweeter because it had gum in it.

Ralph and Sue had three children: Ralph Jr., Samantha, and Barnee. Ralph served his time in the army during the Vietnam War. He was drafted and served in Germany at a munitions dump for two years. Ralph Jr. was born while he was away. After he was born, Sue and little Ralphie went to Germany to be with Ralph. This was in the days before cell phones and email. They would write letters, and sometimes they would send a tape of their voices. We would play it on our cassette player so we could hear them. Mom enjoyed those tapes!

In April of 1980, Ralph was killed in a motorcycle accident. He and a friend were out riding on a very nice Saturday afternoon. Ralph was hit head-on by an oncoming vehicle on a curve. He was killed instantly. Sue came over to tell Mom and Dad the afternoon it happened. This was a very sad day for all of us. Once again, Mom had to turn to Jesus for her strength and help in her time of grief and loss.

LeRoy and Betty were married in July of 1976. They had a big wedding at Grace United Methodist Church. When LeRoy and Betty got married, LeRoy was working for a shoe store in St. Cloud. He soon became the manager of his own store, but it meant they had to move to Muskateen, Iowa. Muskateen was in southern Iowa, along the eastern border. He was there a few years, and then they moved to Iowa Falls, a little closer to home. They had their first boy Brandon in Iowa Falls in 1979. Then they moved to Austin, and then in 1981, they moved back to Foley. They had their second son, Travis, in 1982. Brandon is now married with two boys of his own.

Lisa, that's me, the youngest, and the only girl. I had a lot of problems. First, there was whooping cough when I was only a few weeks old. The doctor believed I wouldn't survive. Then there was a lazy eye and the possibility of scoliosis. There were the trips to the foot doctor for a crooked foot and corrective shoes. Always something wrong with Lisa, Ralph thought at one point maybe Mom should send me back. She didn't like that plan. The lazy eye was probably the worst problem. It had not been discovered until I was in second grade, and by that time it was a little late to correct. My lazy eye is a type of severe astigmatism, one eye does all the work for the other. My right eye was doing all the work, and my left eye was loping along. The standard treatment was to put a patch on the good eye to force the bad eye to work. It usually works pretty well if it is done at an early enough age, in my case, it didn't work.

One day quite a few years later, Mom was talking on the phone, she said she heard God speak to her mind. He told her to take me to see Dr. Gess. Dr. Lowel Gess had been a pastor in Mom and Dad's church before they got married. He and his wife then went to Africa as medical missionaries to help Africans with eye problems, and to share the gospel. He had come back to the United States and set up an office in Alexandria, MN. I was 13 the summer we went to see Dr. Gess. He said there was a new treatment for lazy eyes. He said he would like to try it with me. He had not seen it used on anyone my age, but he thought it was worth a try. At the end of the year, I could read the third line down on the eye chart with my bad eye. When I started, I could not make out the large 'E' at the top. Dr. Gess considered it a success.

Willard, Ellen, Fern, and Walter at a March Birthday Party, sometime in the 1980s.

The Later Years

One milestone in their lives was Walter's retirement. He worked for the railroad for 40 years, starting in the track department and ending up as an equipment operator. When he retired in March of 1981, he was 61. He got to retire early because of his long years of service. He received a good retirement income from the railroad, and Fern got a check too. She was surprised. She asked why she would get a check when she had never worked. The benefits processor told her she had supported her husband by taking care of the family and packing his lunch all those years, so she was entitled to retirement funds as well.

The railroad put on a nice retirement party for Walter at a supper club near Richmond, MN. He and his family were the guests of honor. The officials from the Twin Cities came to his party to congratulate him. This was very unusual. Most of the time when one of the guys retired they had cake and coffee after work in the lunchroom. Walter received the standard retirement gifts and enough money to buy a new recliner. One of the gifts from the local shop was a Tonka backhoe like the one he had operated. It has become one of the grandchildren's favorite toys.

The summer after Walter retired, Fern and Walter went on a second honeymoon trip. They had a single axle Airstream trailer. They hooked it to their car, a 1977 Buick Electra, a nice big car, and they went off to visit all of Walter's brothers and sisters. First to Oregon, to see Wayne Bloom, a nephew, and then Clarence and his family, also living in Oregon. Then they went to California to visit his sister Esther's children, Esther was no longer living. Then on to Arizona to visit Sandy and his family, and then to Texas to visit cousins. They made a stop in Arkansas to visit Walter's sisters, Anna and Martha, and then to Iowa to visit more cousins. Lisa stayed home. She had just graduated from high school and chose not to join them on this trip. They had a really good time. They went on a few other trips after Walter retired. One up through Canada and over to Oregon, this time without the trailer. The first trip was the only long trip they made with the airstream trailer.

Dad had lots of plans for his retirement years. He got a new tiller and started gardening in a big way. He loved the garden, but while he was working he didn't have time for it. Whenever we went to visit we would always have to see how his garden was doing! He also had lots of time to work on other little projects outside. He was always inventing something. I remember after he retired he said he had six Saturdays now. Those years after Walter retired were good years for Fern. She always enjoyed having her family at home.

Tom and Lisa got married in June of 1985. They had their first home in Cloquet, MN, then they moved to Carlton, and finally to Tom's mom's place in Floodwood in 1988 after she died. When they moved to Floodwood, they had a lot of things to sell. They decided to have a garage sale. Mom and Dad knew something about having garage sales, so they came to help out the first year on Labor Day weekend. It turned into an annual event for several years. Fern and Walter would go to garage sales during the summer, buying some things, and cleaning through the things they had. Then they would load up their car and trailer, and come to Floodwood to add their items to our garage sale. We had a good location on a major highway, this meant we had a lot of customers. One year we had over 150 people over the three days of the sale. When Mom and Dad would get to our place, we would have a look at what they brought, and they would see what we had, sometimes we exchanged items before the sale started! One year we had some things from our friends in Floodwood. He was a local police officer. His family went to our church. Mom made some kind of funny remark, John asked Tom where he found her (meaning his mother-in-law). Tom said, "She came with the package." Mom thought it was a good joke!

In January of 1986, Fern and Walter's farmhouse burned. Not to the ground, thankfully, but beyond being able to live in it anymore. The fire started at night. The electronic draft on the wood boiler, in a small room attached to the garage, stuck open and caused the fire to get too hot. Mom woke up and smelled smoke, they turned on the light in the bedroom. The whole room was blue with smoke. Dad told Mom to get dressed, take her purse, and go to the neighbors down the road. They could call the fire department. She did just as he said. It was late at night, about 11:30, and cold outside, but the neighbors were still up. Their neighbor Clyde called the fire department, then went over to Fern and Walter's to help until the fire department arrived. Their farm was about 10 miles out in the country. The Volunteer Fire Department arrived in about 15 minutes to put out the fire before the house was a total loss. The garage and the car however, couldn't be saved. Mom believes God woke her up. They usually went to bed about 9:00 or 9:30, and would not normally wake up. If God hadn't woke her up, the end of this story would be very different. Mom says she will never forget the date. The next day was the day the space shuttle Columbia exploded on take-off.

They were able to live in two rooms of the old house until a new house could be built. They had enough insurance money, just enough, to build a new smaller house. They were able to get a local contractor. He saw their need and got to work as soon as possible, keeping his whole crew on Fern and Walter's house until it was done. They moved into the new house in April, six weeks after construction started. They were able to keep some of the appliances, and most of their personal belongings were salvaged. Fern had a large number of small oil lamps she had collected over the years, none of them were lost. Their family, neighbors, and church friends all pitched in to help them clean up. They also helped them to replace things that were destroyed. Some might say something like this proves it doesn't matter if you serve God all your life, bad things happen anyway. Mom would say, without God in their lives, things would not have come together as quickly, they would not have had as much help, and they would not have weathered the storm nearly as well. Through the bad experience of a house fire, they were able to get a new house to live in for the rest of their retirement years.

Fern is well known in her church for her hugs. She has always had an easy, loving smile, and has always given really good hugs. In the mid 1980's she started her hug ministry. When she went to church on Sunday, she would listen to the Holy Spirit. He would tell her when someone needed a hug. She said often that person would tell her they really needed a hug. She knew it was God using her to comfort and strengthen her church family. Several years ago I wrote this little free verse poem titled "What is a Fern Hug?" Here it is:

> What is a "Fern Hug"?
>
> A "Fern Hug" is love in action.
>
> It costs nothing.
>
> It is available to any who ask.
>
> It is always offered along with a sweet smile.
>
> When you get a "Fern Hug" you know you are loved.
>
> Fern Hugs can be given by anyone,
>
> but they are best when they come from Fern herself.
>
> Thanks, Fern, for showing the love of
>
> Jesus through a simple hug and a smile.

Mom is still giving Fern hugs - or Mom hugs, or Grandma hugs, as the case may be. If you are a part of Fern's family, you cannot go and visit without a hug, or two!

Probably the greatest challenge in Fern's life was when her husband Walter died. He died on a Saturday afternoon on the 22nd of June in 2002. Dad had diabetes for the last 10 years of his life. He was active, and did a lot of walking. He trapped a lot of gophers out in the field.

He liked to walk, and it was good for his diabetes. Walter had not been feeling well for a week or two before that Saturday. Occasionally, he would complain of gas pains. On that Saturday though, he said he was feeling pretty good when he came in for lunch. He sat in his chair after lunch for his noon nap, as was his custom, and then he went outside to work on an old car. A little later he came into the house, Mom took one look at him and said, "You don't feel good, do you?" He said, no. He asked for a cup of water. Just as she brought it to him, he collapsed in her arms. He died of a heart attack that day. Mom said she felt for a pulse at his wrist, and at his neck, but could not feel anything. She knew he was gone. She just prayed, "Jesus, you will have to help me." She said a peace like she has never known came over her. She said she could feel the presence of Jesus with her, and it has never left her.

Mom lives alone now on the farm. But she is not really alone. When she has trouble getting out of the chair because of her arthritic knees, she says, 'Jesus you will have to help me get up', and He does.

She likes to wear a necklace every Sunday. On one Sunday morning, as she was getting ready for church, the chain was all tangled up on the necklace she wanted to wear. She laid it back down and said, "Jesus, you will have to get that untangled if I'm going to wear it." She went to the kitchen. When she came back, the chain was straightened out!

One day a few years ago, she fell. She got her feet tangled up in her walker, and just fell in the kitchen. Just as it happened, her neighbor Clyde was coming in with her mail. Clyde only comes about once a week, while others bring in her mail on other days. He never comes at any particular time. I'm sure God was taking care of Mom that day. Clyde's visit came just when Mom needed him to help her up. Thankfully, she wasn't seriously hurt from the fall. Clyde helped her to stand and got her to her chair.

Fern Sweeter - Mom to some, Grandma to others, Our Dear Fern to friends. The love of God shines through Fern's life. She has belonged to Jesus for 75 years, and He has been her Helper, and her Savior, for all of them. Mom prays daily for her children, grandchildren, and her extended family. She loves all of them, and it shows. She supports her family with her prayers and her encouragement. We all love her a lot, and we know when the day comes that Jesus calls her to her heavenly home, we will miss her. That reminds me of one more story.

One night a few years after Dad died, Mom had a dream. She told me it was so real she wasn't sure she was dreaming. She was outside a large banquet hall. She went into the banquet room, there were lots of tables all set with pretty dishes, it looked like a really nice place. She was looking around the room, and then she saw Walter. He was young with dark hair, and he was healthy. He spotted her across the room. He said, "There you are, I've been waiting for you!" She was so happy to see him again. I am sure it will probably happen just like that one of these days.

And now abide, faith, hope, love. these three; but the greatest of these is love.

I Corinthians 13:13

We love you Mom, Happy 85th Birthday!

The Rest of the Story

In those few months that Mom lived after her 85th birthday, she faced several challenges. In early May, she started having trouble with her eyesight. She was not able to do her handwork like she usually did. She said the TV did not look right to her, although it looked okay to the rest of us. She continued to have this problem until she died. Although she recognized me, she said "You don't look like my Lisa." I believe she was having mini-strokes which were affecting her sight. One day she had an appointment to do some tests to see if there was a problem with her optical nerve. It was a delicate and uncomfortable procedure. She got through it like the trooper she always was. Later I said to her, "You sure did great today." She told me Jesus helped her. She said she sure wished more people would understand how much Jesus would help them if they would only ask.

Toward the end of June, she had a heart attack. She spent a few days in the hospital, but the doctors did not feel they would be able to help her with surgery, so they sent her to a nursing home for rehabilitation. While she was in the nursing home, LeRoy and I visited her regularly, although we could see she was not getting better. She would have good days and bad days.

Finally, the day came when the decision was made to put her on hospice care. I don't think she was on hospice for more than a few weeks. The last time I went to visit her before I left, I asked her if it was okay if I went home. She looked at me for a bit, and then I said again, "Is it okay if I go home to Tom?" She said yes. I told her I loved her, and she told me she loved me too. It was an often repeated exchange between us. She died less than a week later, it was an easy peaceful death. She just went home to heaven, to be with Jesus, Walter, her baby James, and her boy Ralph. What a reunion those of us who know Jesus will have on the day we go to be with our Lord, and our loved ones.

If you don't know Jesus as your Savior, you will not spend eternity with Him. Jesus says in John 14:6, *I am the way, the truth, and the life. No one comes to the Father except through me.* Don't miss out on an eternity with Jesus. Ask Jesus to forgive your sins and be your Savior. If you do, I'm sure you will get to meet Fern in heaven, if you didn't have the privilege of knowing her on earth.

Fern and Walter's Church Directory picture about 2000.

Author's Note

I wrote this book over the winter of 2006-07 in cooperation with Mom. I told her for many years she should write down her stories, but she said, "I can't write!" I said, "Fine, I'll write, you tell me the stories." And that's what we did. I would write a little, and then read what I had written to her. She would tell me if I had something not quite right, or she might tell me another story I had not heard before.

We had a big 85th Birthday party for Mom in March of 2007 when she turned 85. We gave out these stories about her life to her friends and family. It was important to me to preserve some of our family history. This little book certainly does not contain all of her life's story. It does make one thing clear; Mom loved Jesus, her husband, and her family with all her heart, through the good times and the bad times. She was a simple woman who loved deeply. Mom died on August 16, 2007. She is missed by all of us who knew her and loved her.

About the Author:

Lisa Donelson is the youngest child of Fern and Walter Sweeter. She has been writing for many years. She is the author of *Signs of Encouragement*, a devotional based on roadside signs which appeared in the front yard of her home for over 17 years when she and her husband Tom lived in Floodwood, MN.

Lisa and her husband now live in Fargo, ND. She has led several small groups, and enjoys speaking to groups throughout the area. She likes to knit, hold her cat Smokey, (sometimes at the same time!) cook, and read, in her spare time.

Visit Lisa's website to learn more:
https://www.lisadonelson.com

IF YOU ENJOYED THIS BOOK, WILL YOU CONSIDER SHARING IT WITH OTHERS?

- Mention the book in a blog post or through Facebook, Twitter, or Pinterest.

- Pick up a copy for someone you know who would be challenged and encouraged by this message.

www.ingramcontent.com/pod-product-compliance
Lightning Source LLC
Chambersburg PA
CBHW071034080526
44587CB00015B/2610